PHILOSOPHERS OF
THE ENLIGHTENMENT™

MONTESQUIEU

The French Philosopher
Who Shaped
Modern Government

PHILOSOPHERS OF
THE ENLIGHTENMENT ™

MONTESQUIEU

The French Philosopher
Who Shaped
Modern Government

Susan Gordon

The Rosen Publishing Group, Inc., New York

Published in 2006 by The Rosen Publishing Group, Inc.
29 East 21st Street, New York, NY 10010

Copyright © 2006 by The Rosen Publishing Group, Inc.

First Edition

Library of Congress Cataloging-in-Publication Data

Gordon, Susan.
Montesquieu: the French philosopher who shaped modern government / Susan Gordon.—1st ed.
    p. cm.—(Philosophers of the Enlightenment)
Includes bibliographical references.
ISBN 1-4042-0421-0 (library binding)
1. Montesquieu, Charles de Secondat, baron de, 1689–1755—
Criticism and interpretation. 2. Enlightenment—France.
3. France—Intellectual life—18th century.
I. Title. II. Series.
PQ2012.G67 2006
848'.509—dc22

2004028453

Manufactured in Malaysia

On the cover: Background: View of Paris from the eighteenth century. Inset: Portrait of Montesquieu created in 1728.

CONTENTS

This map shows important scientific and academic centers during the eighteenth-century period known as the Enlightenment. The most influential city during the Enlightenment was Paris, France, which was Montesquieu's home for many years of his adult life.

INTRODUCTION

On September 17, 1787, an astounding document was completed that would change the course of world politics and government. This document, the United States Constitution, became the supreme law of the United States of America. Upon its ratification, it unified the thirteen largely separate states to form the new American nation. It created a government based on a complex system of checks and balances in which power would be divided into separate executive, legislative, and judicial branches. This type of government has proven to be a remarkable success. It has stood the test of time and become the model for the governments of several other nations.

James Madison (1751–1836), a driving force behind the U.S. Constitution, cited Charles-Louis de Secondat,

MONTESQUIEU

This portrait of Montesquieu was done in the nineteenth century, many years after Montesquieu had passed away. During his time, Montesquieu was well known as a philosopher and a writer. Today, Montesquieu is best remembered for his contributions to politics and government. His most famous idea, the separation of powers, became an important part of the U.S. Constitution. Montesquieu's influence is still being felt in the United States and democratic nations all over the world.

Baron de Montesquieu (1689–1755) as his authority when he insisted on the separation of powers within the new American government. As he noted in a newspaper article in 1788, "The oracle who is always consulted and cited on [the separation of powers] is the celebrated Montesquieu. If he be not the author of this invaluable precept in the science of politics, he has the merit at least of displaying and recommending it most effectually to the attention of mankind."

The Baron de Montesquieu, or simply Montesquieu (as he is commonly called), was a leading figure in eighteenth-century Europe. This era was called the Enlightenment by the leading philosophers of that time. During this period, philosophers such as Montesquieu examined the society in which they lived and wrote about the different ways they believed it could be improved. Montesquieu became famous for his writings on politics and government. He believed that only through sweeping changes to the government would citizens be able to live free and fulfilled lives.

Montesquieu's World

At the dawn of the eighteenth century, countries throughout Europe were dealing with events that were rapidly changing the world as people had known it for centuries. In response, new ideas emerged concerning science, religion, and government. These new ways of thinking defined the revolutionary period of history known as the Enlightenment.

The Enlightenment was an international movement. Its concepts poured out of France and England and into the far corners of Europe and the United States, reaching Berlin, Rome, Edinburgh, Saint Petersburg, and Philadelphia. Enlightenment intellectuals were critical of all traditions in Europe. They reexamined all political, social, and economic structures as well as ideas about human nature, science, philosophy, morals, and religion.

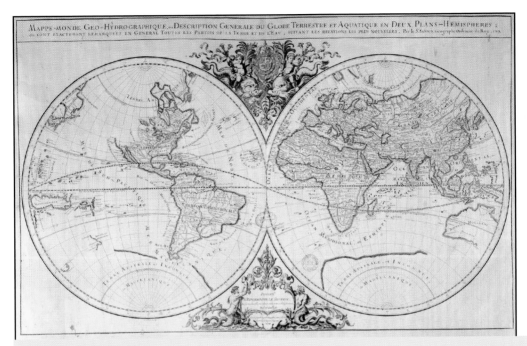

This map was made in France during the Enlightenment. At the time, European explorers had visited and mapped out most of the world, including the entire continents of Asia and Africa. In North America, colonies had been established more than a century earlier, but as evidenced by the area left blank on this map, the western half of the North American continent had not been thoroughly explored.

Enlightenment writers aimed to tear down old structures and rebuild human society. They wanted to build new foundations that rested not in the traditional teachings of the church, but in what was seen as the order of the natural world.

To best understand the goals of Enlightenment leaders, it is important to understand the world in which they were living. During the centuries before the Enlightenment, Europeans had come in contact with parts of the world they had never known before. These areas included North America, South America, and Africa. After discovering these lands, explorers quickly began to set up colonies. Throughout Europe, these new contacts led to people questioning their views of the world. These views were centuries old and were based on religion or the words of kings and queens as the source of truth. The discoveries made by sixteenth-century movements such as the scientific revolution and the Protestant Reformation persuaded more and more people to move away from these traditional sources of knowledge.

THE RENAISSANCE

The Renaissance was the period of European history roughly from the fourteenth century into the seventeenth century. This political, artistic, and scientific movement was based on a rediscovery of ideas that were popular during the empires of Greece and Rome. The Renaissance marked a move away from the church as the most influential force within society. Instead, the individual became the basis for social and political systems. In this way, the Renaissance marked a transition from the medieval to the modern era. This transition would be completed during the era that followed the Renaissance—the Enlightenment. In this era,

THE LIGHT

Throughout history, light has been used as a symbol of wisdom. Enlightenment intellectuals believed that humankind used wisdom, or light, as a way to advance out of the Dark Ages of history. In France, the period of the Enlightenment is known as *le siècle des lumières*, which means "the century of light."

concepts we sometimes take for granted today, such as liberty and democracy, came to the forefront.

THE ROADS LEADING TO ENLIGHTENMENT

Well into the seventeenth century, bitter and bloody religious wars were being fought among European Christians in the wake of the Protestant Reformation. These wars devastated the foundations of European countries. Depending on their own religious and political beliefs, monarchs would force their subjects to convert to Catholicism or to become Protestants. Often, the subjects would resist, leading

During the sixteenth century, people who held religious beliefs different from those in power risked being accused of witchcraft. As punishment, the accused witches were sometimes burned alive. Witch burnings occurred most often in countries, such as Germany, where Protestants and Catholics were at odds with each other.

to numerous government-backed witch burnings, revolts, and, eventually, full-scale wars.

In addition, with the Renaissance curiosity about the surrounding world, explorers and missionaries began to push farther and farther into non-European lands. Here they came into contact with many religions for the first time. The ideas of major Eastern religions such as Hinduism, Buddhism, and Confucianism became subjects that brought both fascination and fear to many Europeans. Also, trade relations with the Ottoman Empire (modern Turkey),

Depicted above is the siege of Constantinople. For many centuries, Constantinople was one of the largest and most important cities in the world. It was located in what is today the country of Turkey. On May 29, 1453, Constantinople fell to the Ottoman Empire, a powerful Muslim state, and was renamed Istanbul.

which practiced Islam, exposed Europeans to Islam, which posed a threat to traditional beliefs.

CULTURES CLASH IN THE RENAISSANCE

During the Renaissance, answers to political and religious questions were based on asserting the truth of one viewpoint over another. If the use of force became necessary, the thinking went, then so be it. Christian Europe and the Muslims in the East clashed regularly. European Jews were regularly subjected to harassment and violence, and forced to leave their countries. The Protestant criticism of Catholic doctrine led to widespread condemnation of the Catholic clergy and to the breakup of the Jesuits, a scholarly branch of the Catholic Church.

The need to address these tensions would lead to the development of several principles of Enlightenment thought. The call for separation of church and state, for religious tolerance, and for freedom from censorship by church authorities were all Enlightenment solutions to the problems eighteenth-century Europe had inherited from previous eras.

THE ENLIGHTENMENT BEGINS

In early eighteenth-century Europe, a new way of thinking arose in response to centuries of war, persecution, and tyranny. This new era, termed the Enlightenment by its founders, marked a fundamental shift in how people felt about their place in society. Enlightenment thought was based on an absolute faith in the power of human reason to solve basic problems of existence.

Enlightenment thinkers stressed individual self-determination and human equality, and valued the ability to reason over blind faith. The idea of progress, of movement from one way of life to an improved

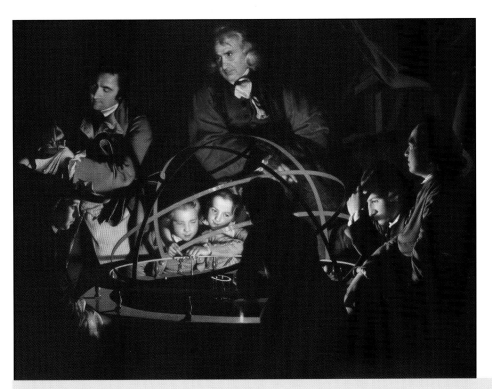

This painting from 1766 is entitled *A Philosopher Giving a Lecture on the Orrery*. An orrery is a model that shows the positions of the planets and stars in a solar system. During the Enlightenment, scientists published books and educated many people about the wonders of the natural world. This was in stark contrast to previous centuries, when scientific inquiry was heavily censored by the Catholic Church.

one, is a basic Enlightenment concept. Enlightenment ideals, born in French intellectual circles, quickly spread through Europe as a general movement away from religious superstitions. Religion took on a complex role in Enlightenment thought. Since nature was created by God, observation of nature could provide man with insight into the mind of God and, therefore, into the basic truths of the world. Enlightenment thinkers believed that the ability to examine the natural order of the universe was the most important

THE BOOK OF HUMAN KNOWLEDGE

An important Enlightenment project was Denis Diderot's *Encyclopedia*. This book was published in France in installments from 1751 to 1772. Diderot was the book's main editor. A number of other important Enlightenment figures contributed to the project, including Montesquieu, Voltaire, Jean Le Rond d'Alembert, and Jean-Jacques Rousseau.

In the *Encyclopedia*, Diderot gathered information on a diverse range of subjects, much like the encyclopedias of today. This collection of writings and illustrations was an attempt to organize all human knowledge according to rational observation. The writers of the *Encyclopedia* saw it as a reaction against superstitious thought that had been encouraged by the church and the government of France for centuries.

The *Encyclopedia* served as a summary of Enlightenment thought. In France at that time, however, it caused a great deal of controversy. This was mostly due to its ideas on religious tolerance, its support for Protestant leaders, and its challenges of the Catholic Church. The entire work was banned by the French monarchy, but the *Encyclopedia*'s supporters found a way around that. They sold the work by subscription and delivered it secretly to the subscribers.

feature of human existence and should be the basis for all social and political institutions.

Enlightenment leaders favored new styles of government. Traditional aristocracies and rule by kings and queens who claimed to be appointed by God were to be replaced by republics and democracies. Before the Enlightenment, religious leaders and monarchs decided how people should behave in society, but now rational thinking would lead all citizens of a republic naturally to a sense of civic duty and honor. These new worldviews, it was thought, would prevent the violence that had torn Europe apart for so long.

POLITICAL QUESTIONS

The search for the nature of existence and the best ways to organize a society led to increasingly complex questions. How should power be distributed in a government? Should the right to govern be given to one person or shared by groups of people? What form should those groups take? Was the government above the law or subject to it? What made a law legitimate? What was the best way of organizing society to ensure that it would be stable and work for the good of all? In answering these questions, Enlightenment thinkers often referred to Christian morals and ideas, but they remained committed to keeping political power and religious institutions separate.

After years of persecution and many lives lost in the name of religious beliefs, the Enlightenment's most important task was to find ways of changing existing political structures in order to prevent further chaos and violence. The relations between church and government demanded the most attention. Rational thinking was said to be the solution to the problems created by blind faith in religion. As appealing as this view was to people who were tired of religious conflict and intolerance, it raised many serious questions about the moral qualities of the world.

To Enlightenment thinkers, upholding moral standards was extremely important. If religion could no longer serve as the source of morality, then moral instructions needed to be found elsewhere. Enlightenment thinkers asked many questions: Did the good, the beautiful, and the true exist in the world as real things? Were they relative to time, place, and person? What was the origin of moral behavior in human beings? What should people be allowed to do? And what should they not be allowed to do? Much of the writing produced by Enlightenment philosophers attempted to answer these questions.

LITERATURE OF THE ENLIGHTENMENT

The Enlightenment was essentially a movement created by writers. The leaders of this movement often relied on the written word to explore and broadcast their values. One Enlightenment goal was to create new forms of fiction and journalism in order to spread Enlightenment ideals. The novel developed as the most appropriate form of fiction for this goal. It immediately became immensely popular.

The novel had existed in seventeenth-century France, but at that time it was seen as an amateur art form that anyone could master. However, in the early eighteenth century, the growing and literate middle-class population in England began to demand materials that would address its concerns and sensibilities. The novel, with its potential for intricate plots and well-developed characters,

SPREADING ENLIGHTENMENT IDEAS

The Enlightenment was an intellectual movement that spread through social gatherings and events. This social component set the Enlightenment apart from preceding eras. People who were committed to the cause tended to gather together to discuss their ideas. Often, intellectuals and other well-known members of society would gather at events known as salons. These events were popular in the elegant living rooms and apartments of wealthy and educated residents across Paris.

Depicted above is a ceremony of the secret society known as the Freemasons. In the eighteenth century, Freemasons often gathered to discuss philosophy and current events.

Coffeehouses were another popular gathering place. Here, aristocrats could mingle openly with educated commoners and further spread Enlightenment ideals.

Articles and editorials in journals, magazines, and newspapers, scientific societies, political clubs, reading clubs and lending libraries, as well as secret societies such as the Freemasons and Bavarian Illuminati further helped to develop and spread these new theories.

appealed to this mindset. The novel would provide the new middle class with what its members wanted to read most: stories about ordinary characters dealing with the growing complexity of contemporary life.

The new literary form spread throughout Europe. A particularly popular genre was fictional travel literature. Fictional travel literature addressed contemporary European life by using imaginary characters and locations as substitutes for real European situations. Writers could criticize those imaginary places and people (which readers could easily recognize as representations of their world) and avoid any penalty that might arise from criticizing real people and places. *Persian Letters* (1721) by Montesquieu is an outstanding example of fictional travel literature.

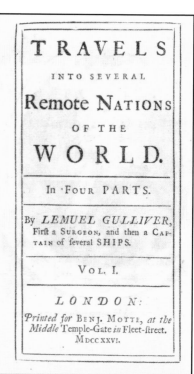

Pictured above is the frontispiece and title page of *Travels Into Several Remote Nations of the World*, which was published in 1729 and is commonly known as *Gulliver's Travels*. The author is listed as Lemuel Gulliver, an English sea captain. In reality, the author was an Englishman named Jonathan Swift. The book was an imitation of the popular travel literature of the day, which often described exotic lands that had recently been discovered. Swift's book, however, described the countries of Lilliput and Brobdingnag, which were not real countries, but inventions of the author.

Its tale of two Persian noblemen visiting Paris, and their faraway Persian world, gives an extensive look at both Europe and the East. The book satisfied the growing European interest in the cultures of other parts of the world. With the advent of the novel, reading soon became a favorite pastime throughout enlightened Europe.

THE BARON DE MONTESQUIEU

Charles-Louis de Secondat, Baron de Montesquieu, was one of the greatest French figures of the Enlightenment. He was a prolific writer known for his intelligence as well as his calm, moderate approach to life. His easygoing personality, which is evident in his writings, is also reflected through the events in his rather quiet life.

THE EARLY YEARS

Charles-Louis was born on January 18, 1689, at his family's castle of La Brède in southwestern France. His father, Jacques de Secondat, and his mother, Marie-Françoise de Pesnel, both came from wealthy and well-respected families.

Tragedy struck Charles-Louis at a young age. When he was seven years old, his mother died. For the next four

Seen above is Montesquieu's birthplace and home for many years, the castle of La Brède. The castle, known as a château in French, was built in the fifteenth century and still stands today. It is situated in the heart of France's wine country. Wines from this region are among the most expensive in the world.

years, he was raised by his father. Then at age eleven, as was the custom with noble families, the young Charles-Louis went to live among the peasants in the village of La Brède. His country upbringing had a profound effect on him. Throughout his life, Montesquieu would remain loyal to his rustic roots. He spoke with an accent unique to the Gascony region. And although he was to travel extensively throughout his life, he would always find some time to return to La Brède—the only place where he truly felt at home.

The Seine River as it passes through Paris is the focus of this eighteenth-century engraving. In Montesquieu's time, Paris was the political and cultural center of France, even as it is today. Montesquieu spent many years of his adult life in Paris, where he enjoyed the company of an international crowd of aristocrats and intellectuals.

In 1700, Charles-Louis was sent to the Oratorian Collège de Juilly, one of the most prestigious schools in France. He returned to Bordeaux in 1705 to study law, and in 1708 he was admitted to the Bordeaux parliament as a lawyer. He spent the next five years in Paris. During this period, he had a chance to observe Parisian society, which he later ridiculed in *Persian Letters*, his first successful book.

MARRIAGE

In 1715, Montesquieu married Jeanne de Lartigue, who brought him a large dowry. Jeanne was a devout Calvinist (someone who practices Calvinism, a

Protestant faith). When Louis XIV—the king of France during Montesquieu's time—overturned a law that protected religious freedom, Lartigue refused to renounce her faith, risking imprisonment. Her political and religious convictions appealed to Montesquieu, who felt strongly about people's right to practice the religion of their choice.

In the same year he married Lartigue, Montesquieu was elected to the Bordeaux Academy of Sciences. The following year, 1716, his uncle died, leaving him the title of Baron de Montesquieu. He also inherited his uncle's entire fortune and an extremely important judicial seat: presidency of the Bordeaux parliament.

Although Montesquieu kept a polite relationship with his wife, their marriage was not a very romantic one. She was not well educated, and he seems to have thought of her as a plain and boring companion, although he did consider her an efficient and hardworking partner. Once married, Montesquieu kept up his travels. He visited the leading intellectual figures of England, Germany, and Italy, and maintained his own apartment in Paris. In the meantime, Lartigue stayed in Gascony, managing the castle and vineyards of La Brède. Together they had three children.

Certain aspects of Montesquieu were contradictory. He retained his country roots and mannerisms while feeling very much at home in the salons of cosmopolitan Paris. He was a product of the old French aristocratic world, but he also admired and yearned for the bourgeois, or middle-class, lifestyle he would soon discover in England. Despite his later call for legal equality for all, Montesquieu always retained his aristocratic tendencies. This would lead him to do things that appear cruel and unfair to us today. For example, in order to maintain the family's noble lineage and wealth, Montesquieu forced his daughter Denise to marry a much older third cousin. However, it must be noted that back then, this was not something uncommon for a father to do—especially one of Montesquieu's elite social status.

EARLY CAREER

Montesquieu divided his time among his work as a judge, his activities as a winemaker and merchant, and his work for the Bordeaux Academy of Sciences. Law, commerce, and science, all important parts of his life, helped shape his political theories. In 1721, Montesquieu left his post as president of the

Montesquieu is seen at his writing table in this illustration. Montesquieu was a patient and determined writer, often rewriting material numerous times until he considered it ready for publication. His masterpiece, *The Spirit of the Laws* was more than 1,000 pages long.

parliament of Bordeaux. He retained, however, the title of Monsieur le President throughout his life.

THE WRITER

In 1721, Montesquieu shook the European literary world with *Persian Letters*. (Its original French name was *Lettres Persanes*.) The book's combination of juicy gossip, exotic settings, and insightful criticism of contemporary French society made it an instant success. But because of its open critique of European society, it was also a scandalous work. As a result, when Montesquieu applied for admission into the prestigious French Academy, he was denied entry.

Montesquieu decided to move to Paris shortly after the publication of *Persian Letters*. In Paris, he led an extremely active social and intellectual life. In 1728, the French Academy finally admitted him as a member. In 1728, Montesquieu also spent time in the Hapsburg Empire (now Austria and Hungary) and parts of Italy. During this trip, he began pondering the themes that would later take shape in his two great philosophical histories: *Considerations on the Causes of the Greatness of the Romans and Their Decline* (1734) and *The Spirit of the Laws* (1748).

From 1729 until 1731, Montesquieu lived in England, where he joined various societies and became an active participant in British political life. His observations of the British parliamentary form of government gave Montesquieu the direction to finish his most famous work. This book, *The Spirit of the Laws*, was published in 1748, seventeen years after his visit to England. He spent more than twenty years working on it. This book was an enormous success throughout Europe. Within two years, twenty-two editions—including translations into every major European language—were published.

Once *The Spirit of the Laws* was published, Montesquieu, whose eyesight had been steadily declining, returned to La Brède. Although he was almost totally blind, he continued to write and do

CONSIDÉRATIONS
SUR LES CAUSES
DE LA
GRANDEUR
DES
ROMAINS,
ET DE LEUR
DÉCADENCE.

Nouvelle Edition, revue, corrigée &
augmentée par l'Auteur.

'A laquelle on a joint un DIALOGUE DE SYLLA
ET D'EUCRATE.

A PARIS, RUE S. JACQUES,
Chez HUART & MOREAU fils, Libraires de LA
REINE & Libraires-Imprimeurs de Monseigneur
LE DAUPHIN, à la Justice & au grand Saint
Basile.

M. DCC. XLVIII.

as much research as he could. On February 10, 1755, he died.

At the time of his death, Montesquieu was so famous and admired that the French Jesuits and the group of philosophers close to Montesquieu publicly argued over who would preside over his last moments of life. The Jesuits claimed that shortly before his death he had repented of his sins and had returned to the arms of the Catholic Church. The philosophers denied the Jesuits' claims and insisted that their colleague had remained true to his anti-church ideals to the end.

MONTESQUIEU'S MANNERS

Montesquieu's down-to-earth, practical view of society and government was due not only to his studies, travels, and observations, but also in

Considerations on the Causes of the Greatness of the Romans and Their Decline (Considérations sur les Causes de la Grandeur des Romains et de Leur Décadence) was published in 1734. The title page pictured at left is from an edition published in Paris in 1748. *Considerations* was Montesquieu's first great book of political philosophy. In the book, he discusses the lessons that political leaders can learn from the mistakes made by the leaders of the Roman Empire (circa 31 BC–AD 476).

large part to his calm and moderate personality. He found intense emotions of any kind to be distasteful. Emotions such as passion, love, and anger were of no interest to him. In fact, he was known to remark that a person displaying such strong emotions was just like any other person displaying those same emotions. In contrast, he said, the world of ideas offered endless variety and excitement.

THE INSPIRATION OF PARIS

The world of ideas that made Montesquieu so happy was based in Paris. Montesquieu and his contemporaries took great pride in getting together to discuss the latest in politics, arts, science, and philosophy. Because Paris was the intellectual center of Europe, Montesquieu was able to converse with many of the most influential thinkers of the period.

Even among the finest European minds, Montesquieu stood out as both an original thinker and an embodiment of a man of the Enlightenment. He was well respected by fellow philosophers and writers. His goal was to devise a system that would ensure a society with greater freedom for its people. Freedom, Montesquieu believed, would allow people to express their naturally curious and creative qualities. A free society would be able to advance in ways unimaginable during the centuries of rule by the church and its allies.

THE BARON AND THE KING

Montesquieu was born in France during the age of King Louis XIV (1638–1715). The reign

This portrait of Louis XIV of France was created in the late seventeenth century. Because Louis was only five years old when he became king, his mother, Anne of Austria, ruled for him until 1651. At that time, he was considered old enough to rule on his own.

of Louis XIV (1643–1715), from the palace of Versailles, was the longest in European history, and it was a central influence on Montesquieu's ideas. Louis XIV was a generous patron of the arts and is known as the Sun King because of the artistic and architectural brilliance of his world-famous palace.

During his reign, Louis XIV reformed many outdated and corrupt aspects of his father's government. For example, he instituted a system of royal assessment of government officials, who could now be removed from office if they failed to perform their public duties. Early in his reign he worked to improve the French criminal justice system and commerce and tax-collection system. He also reduced the French national debt.

Louis XIV was a great patron of the arts. He supported many of the greatest French literary and artistic figures of his time. He founded scholarship and art academies, and he took control of the French Academy, of which Montesquieu would become a member. Under his rule, the Louvre Museum was built in Paris, and the famous Palace of Versailles, which became the home of the Sun King's court in 1682, was built on the grounds of his father's old hunting lodge.

Louis XIV was also a successful war leader and won many new territories for the kingdom of France. With these conquests, however, he grew more and more arrogant and dictatorial, especially during the later years of his rule. In 1680, he created a legal system that allowed him to simply declare that various towns and villages were

Louis XIV hosted lavish events at the Palace of Versailles to which the most important citizens of France were invited. The ornate decorations and opulence of the palace's interior can be seen in this painting by Eugene Lami from the mid-nineteenth century. The painting is entitled, appropriately, *Big Party at the Palace of Versailles*.

suddenly French territories. His wars were also very costly, and over the years, those costs devastated the French economy.

In 1715, after more than seventy years of ruling France, King Louis XIV found himself with little control over his administration. It had become useless and inefficient and did more harm than good for the people of France. On September 1, 1715, the Sun King died, leaving the people of France with problems and tensions that demanded immediate solutions.

THE BARON'S IDEAS ON MONARCHY

King Louis XIV was an absolute monarch. Absolutism, a specific form of monarchy in which the king or queen has unlimited power, was an important political concept in Europe during the Enlightenment. The idea of absolute rule retained its appeal for some of the Enlightenment's observers of eighteenth-century politics, but eventually most Enlightenment thinkers abandoned their support of absolutism. They called instead for some form of limited monarchy or representative government. In the early nineteenth century, the term "absolutism" began to imply tyrannical rule as well, but this was not the case during Montesquieu's time. Although the absolute monarch ruled as the supreme leader, he or she could not abuse his or her power. Rather, the monarch was bound to follow the fundamental laws of the land and the laws of God. If such a monarch disregarded those fundamental laws, he or she was no longer an absolute ruler, but a despot, or, in modern terms, a dictator. Despotism was the name given to such a government.

For Montesquieu, despotism was a real nightmare that had plagued France during the reign of King Louis XIV. Montesquieu was above all concerned with finding a form of government that could ensure the end of despotism.

THE BOOKS

Montesquieu sought to understand how law shaped politics and society. His books are explorations of what causes and what prevents despotic, or tyrannical, governments. During the eighteenth century, his ideas, especially as expressed in *The Spirit of the Laws*, were widely praised and imitated. In many countries, such as England and Germany, Montesquieu was the best known and most influential of the French writers of the Enlightenment. In the North American colonies, he provided inspiration and criticism to a new world that was still trying to define itself.

PERSIAN LETTERS

Because not much happened in Montesquieu's personal life, there is not a lot of literature on the man himself. In contrast, the writings of Montesquieu offer a wealth of material from which to choose.

His most famous and influential works are *The Spirit of the Laws* and *Persian Letters*. In addition to those books, he wrote a collection of scientific memoirs on diverse topics such as the functions of the kidneys, coal mining, the ebb and flow of the sea, and the physical history of Earth. He explored economic questions in *Considerations on the Wealth of Spain* (1726), political history in *Considerations on the Causes of the Greatness of the Romans and Their Decline*, and aesthetics in *The Essay on Taste* (1755). He also wrote travel stories, imaginary interviews, reviews, and even a museum catalog.

TALES OF EXOTIC LANDS

In the early eighteenth century, literature about exotic places was extremely popular. Montesquieu, like many others at the time, spent a large amount of time reading works such as *Arabian Nights*, a classic collection of Middle Eastern folk tales. This reading, combined with Montesquieu's critical attitude toward contemporary life, led him to write the first of his great works, *Persian Letters*.

THE STORY

Persian Letters, one of the earliest and most famous European novels, was a satirical novel published in 1721. Although it was published anonymously, the identity of its author, Montesquieu, was well known. Censorship in France made it necessary to publish *Persian Letters* in Amsterdam, but the book was smuggled into France. There it became a best seller and earned Montesquieu international fame.

    Persian Letters is a novel that is written in the form of letters, also known as an epistolary novel. This was one of the most popular eighteenth-century forms of fiction. *Persian Letters* consists of letters written by two imaginary young men from Persia (modern-day Iran) to their wives and friends back

Pictured above is a nineteenth-century illustration from *Arabian Nights*. The book, also known as *The Book of One Thousand and One Nights*, is a collection of Middle Eastern folk tales. In these stories, Western audiences were first introduced to the legends of Aladdin, Sinbad the Sailor, and Ali Baba and the forty thieves. The book was extremely popular throughout Europe during Montesquieu's time.

home. In these letters the two young men, Usbek and Rica, criticize and mock the laws and morals of Paris society. Through Usbek, Montesquieu is able to criticize the king of France and the pope. He accuses the two leaders of tricking and forcing people into doing and believing things they would normally refuse to do and think. The following example is from Letter 24, in which Usbek

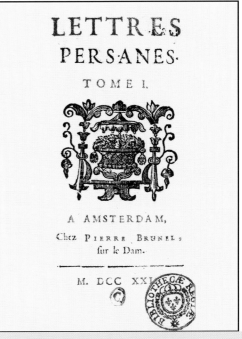

Montesquieu's *Persian Letters* was published in 1721. The novel was critical of both French society and Persian society. The title page seen above is from the first edition of the book, published in Amsterdam.

writes to Ibben, his friend back home, and tries to make sense of the French political system.

The king of France is the most powerful of European potentates. He has no mines of gold like his neighbour, the king of Spain; but he is much wealthier than that prince; because his riches are drawn from a more inexhaustible source, the vanity of his subjects. He has undertaken and carried on great wars, without any other supplies than those derived from the sale of titles of honour; and it is by a prodigy of human pride that his troops are paid, his towns fortified, and his fleets equipped.

Then again, the king is a great magician, for his dominion extends to the minds of his subjects; he makes them think what he wishes. If he has only a million crowns in his exchequer, and has need of two million, he has only to persuade them that one crown is worth two, and they believe it. If he has a costly war on hand, and is short of money, he simply suggests to his subjects that a piece of paper is coin of the realm, and they are straightway convinced of it. He has even succeeded in persuading them that his touch is a sovereign cure for all sorts of diseases, so great is the power and influence he has over their minds.

Despite his criticism of the French king, Montesquieu's preference for the West remains clear throughout *Persian Letters*. He takes a far more critical view of Usbek and Rica's world in the East. Along with these two characters' letters describing the

In this illustration from Montesquieu's *Persian Letters*, a Persian man is seen having a conversation with a Capuchin monk. The Capuchins formed a missionary organization within the Catholic Church. Their goal was to spread the beliefs of the church and recruit new church members. The comparison of two different cultures, illustrated here with the European monk and the Persian man, was one of the main themes of *Persian Letters*.

peculiar and irrational ways of the West are letters written by their wives from their harem back home. The letters of the wives illustrate a way of life that is vastly more alarming to readers than anything Usbek and Rica have seen in the West. Usbek, the mild-mannered Persian gentleman visiting Paris salons, is a despot in his own harem; he wields the power to preserve or destroy life over women who exist only to satisfy his every desire. While Usbek's letters to his wives are entertaining observations on the ways of Christian infidels, the women's letters are angry, jealous, and rebellious outbursts. Zelis, a wife whom Usbek orders punished for disobeying him, sends him the following letter (Letter 158):

You are a thousand leagues from me, and yet you condemn me! A thousand leagues from me, and yet you punish me!

When a barbarous eunuch lays his vile hands upon me, it is by your order: it is the tyrant who outrages me, and not the instrument of his tyranny.

You may, if you choose, redouble your cruel treatment. My heart is at peace, since it can no longer love you. Your soul is debased, and you have become cruel. Rest assured that you are not beloved. Farewell.

The book ends melodramatically when Roxana, Usbek's favorite wife, kills herself in an act of rebellion against the husband who is unable to see her and the world as they really are. The last letter of the book, Letter 161, is the suicide note from Roxana.

How could you think that I was such a weakling as to imagine there was nothing for me in the world but to worship your caprices; that while you indulged all your desires, you should have the right to thwart me in all mine? No: I have lived in slavery, and yet always retained my freedom: I have remodeled your laws upon those of nature; and my mind has always maintained its independence.

. . . Doubtless such a letter as this you little expected to receive. Can it be possible that after having overwhelmed you with affliction I shall still force you to admire my courage? But all is ended now; the poison destroys me, my strength leaves me, my pen drops from my hand; even my hate grows weaker: I die.

Montesquieu's description of this last act, as well as the harem system of many wives, was meant

Baghdad, Iraq, is seen from a distance in this eighteenth-century engraving. By comparing this image with the image of Paris on page 27, we can get a good idea of the difference between Eastern and Western cities. For many centuries of its turbulent history, Baghdad was part of Persia. In 1638, it came under control of the Ottoman Empire. Not until after World War I did Iraq become an independent nation.

to illustrate what he saw as the illogical and irrational behavior of the East.

THEMES IN *PERSIAN LETTERS*

Montesquieu's critique of Persian society in his novel had two sides to it. Usbek's harem in Persia was also a symbol for the French court and for the religious life of Catholic monasteries and nunneries, which he

This painting from the eighteenth century shows two Persian women embroidering a rug. The painting was done by Charles-Andre Van Loo, a Frenchman. It is likely the painter never visited Persia, but instead based his depiction on stories he had read or other paintings he had seen. In the eighteenth century, a Persian rug was considered to be among the finest of its kind and prized throughout Europe.

saw as examples of the oppression and cruelty that inevitably come from any type of irrational behavior.

Persian Letters deals with the theme of unhappiness, which Montesquieu sees as the result of unreasonable human institutions and laws. In the book, the laws of the harem dictate that Usbek's wives cannot take other lovers, but must remain faithful to him. However, this law only applies to the women of the harem and not to Usbek, who is allowed to do whatever he pleases. This unreasonable system leads to extreme unhappiness and even suicide by one of the wives. Montesquieu's great achievement with this novel was that he was able to write a witty and engaging story that also carried an important message. This message was that in order to last, society must be built on virtue and fairness.

BEYOND *PERSIAN LETTERS*

Although it remains a highly entertaining and amusing book, *Persian Letters* takes a pessimistic view of human nature. Not until Montesquieu encountered the English government and way of life, seven years after the publication of *Persian Letters*, would his vision of the world change. The result of this new outlook would be *The Spirit of the Laws*.

THE SPIRIT OF THE LAWS

1
2
3
4
5
6

CHAPTER 4

Throughout his numerous and varied works, Montesquieu concentrates on the same themes. Again and again, observations, questions, and answers dealing with the nature of the individual and the effect of historical events surfaced in his writings. In 1748, Montesquieu would express these thoughts masterfully in *The Spirit of the Laws*, the most important and influential book of his entire career.

THE BARON AND THE CLASSICAL WORLD

Although he had studied law and practiced in the French courts for more than a decade, Montesquieu had no great enthusiasm for law as a profession. He was much more interested in how the laws had come

DE L'ESPRIT

DES

LOIX,

Ou du rapport que les Loix doivent avoir avec la Constitution de chaque Gouvernement, les Moeurs,
le Climat, la Religion, le Commerce, &c.

à quoi l'Auteur a ajoûté

Des recherches nouvelles sur les Loix Romaines, touchant les Suc-
cessions, sur les Loix Françoises, & sur les Loix Féodales.

NOUVELLE EDITION.

*Corrigée par l'Auteur, & augmentée d'une Table des Matieres, & d'une
Carte Géographique, pour servir à l'intelligence des articles
qui concernent le Commerce.*

PREMIERE PARTIE.

.... *Prolem sine matre creatam.* Ovid.

par M. de Montesquieu

A GENEVE,

Chez BARRILLOT & FILS.

M. DCC. XLIX.

to be and how they reflected the needs and fears of society. *The Spirit of the Laws* developed from this interest and was the second of his two great books on political philosophy.

The first book, *Considerations on the Causes of the Greatness of the Romans and Their Decline*, never achieved the popularity of *The Spirit of the Laws*, but it outlined what would become one of Montesquieu's main topics in his more famous work. *Considerations* claimed that the greatness of the Roman Empire was due to its citizens' virtues and to its political and legal institutions, which were flexible and could adapt to meet the needs of the people. In this book, Montesquieu explained how Rome's failure to maintain these features led to its tyrannical government, which he then pinpointed as the cause of the empire's collapse.

Montesquieu's masterpiece, *The Spirit of the Laws* (De L'Esprit des Loix), was published in 1748. The book contained many influential political theories, such as his belief that a government should not be overly rigid, but should be flexible so that it can adapt to change. The book also served to educate people in France and throughout Europe about the English system of government, which Montesquieu admired very much. At left is a 1749 edition of the book, published in Geneva, Switzerland.

MONTESQUIEU'S LAWS

Fourteen years after publishing his study of Rome, Montesquieu brought his search for the best forms of government to completion with *The Spirit of the Laws*. It was completed in 1743 and published anonymously in Geneva in 1748, after twenty years of writing and research. *The Spirit of the Laws* is Montesquieu's masterpiece. In it, he describes how the environment, social relationships, and history of every country affect that country's system of government. In the following passage from the book, he introduces the idea of laws as being defined by their subjects.

> Laws, in their most general signification, are the necessary relations arising from the nature of things. In this sense all beings have their laws: the Deity His laws, the material world its laws, the intelligences superior to man their laws, the beasts their laws, man his laws.

Within the more than 600 chapters divided across thirty-one volumes, Montesquieu redefined law as the necessary relationships that are derived from nature. Laws, he said, had their most basic political expression in government. Furthermore, he claimed, although such a relationship was the same anywhere and under any conditions, actual laws needed to accurately reflect the people they were meant to serve. He saw this as a natural, desirable condition and a flexible government as the kind best suited to that condition. Furthermore, he presented the separation of powers as the best way of establishing and protecting the freedom to which every citizen was naturally entitled.

Although French censors never gave the book official approval, *The Spirit of the Laws* was available throughout France and was an immediate success.

THE IDEAS BEHIND THE BOOK

A common Enlightenment concept was that of natural law. Natural law is defined as the law that comes from nature and is the standard for judging human actions. Using the concept of natural law, Montesquieu outlined a basic doctrine of human rights. The basic duty of government was to protect such rights. Montesquieu saw governments that could not do

A CATHOLIC CENTER OF ENLIGHTENMENT

Rome began changing dramatically in the late sixteenth century as the Catholic Church responded to the Protestant Reformation. This period of history is known as the Counter-Reformation. The Baroque style in art and architecture that developed in Rome at the time is one of the hallmarks of the Counter-Reformation. Baroque art and architecture beautified the city of Rome. Immense, splendidly decorated palaces were built to emphasize the extent of papal power. The hope was that this grand display would convince people of the superiority of the Catholic Church over any Protestant church.

Above is the Palazzo Senatorio (Palace of the Senate) in Rome, an example of early baroque architecture. Originally built in the Middle Ages, the exterior of the Palazzo was redone in the late sixteenth century.

During the Enlightenment, Rome served as a major cultural center in Europe. The city that had once served as the capital of the great Roman Empire now inspired people to revive the ideals of that ancient world. Artists, architects, writers, and musicians flocked to the vibrant city in order to study and improve their craft. Young, wealthy Europeans nearly always included Rome on the itineraries of their grand tours. In short, the city was a source of fascination for minds of the Enlightenment, serving as a symbol of both good and bad institutions and events.

this as holding illegal claim to power. According to Montesquieu, political power needed to be grounded in something other than brute force. Laws, which had for so long been rooted in the ideas of the church, were now seen as based in the rational laws observable in the real world. This would be the basis for his new idea of government, in which reason, instead of blind faith in tradition, became the glue that would hold society together.

Creating new types of government—a major goal of the Enlightenment—required answers to new questions about individual freedom and social responsibilities. Do people retain any individual freedom when they live in a society? If they do enjoy such freedom, is it limited to any extent? What are the specific obligations of government? Although the preferred form varied from country to country, Enlightenment thinkers supported the following styles of government: liberal individualism (in which the individual is basically governed by his or her own reason), Enlightenment forms of despotism (in which monarchs use their authority for the good of their subjects), and direct democracy (in which the people all participate directly in their government).

THE SOCIAL CONTRACT

A fundamental contribution of the Enlightenment to modern political thought is social contract theory. According to this theory, the ultimate power, or sovereignty, over a society is held by the people. In creating the social contract, people give some power to a designated authority, trading some of their freedom for security. Originally, there was disagreement over whether the contract gives absolute sovereignty to that designated authority or to the people. Eventually, thinkers agreed that the original foundation of society involves an agreement by the people to give up some independence in return for the protection offered by a government. The resulting governments could take any of several forms, including a monarchy or a democracy.

In addressing such issues, Montesquieu came out on a firm middle ground. As a member of the French aristocracy, he believed that the aristocracy could best protect the

Thomas Hobbes (1588–1679) was an English philosopher well known for his ideas on the social contract theory. Like Montesquieu, he wrote extensively about politics and government.

state from giving way to oppression, whether at the hands of a monarch (tyranny) or at the hands of the people (anarchy). He argued that freedom could best be preserved by balancing the claims of absolute monarchs against democratic demands. The nobility could serve as a mediator between these two forces, ensuring that neither could gain enough power to be a threat to freedom. His preferred form of government, modeled after his

Fashionable aristocrats gather for wine and conversation in this engraving from the eighteenth century. Montesquieu enjoyed gatherings such as these, where he could discuss current events and new philosophical ideas. This picture shows the glamorous side of French society. The majority of French people in the eighteenth century were poor farmers or tradesmen who would not have attended any event such as this.

understanding of the English system, was based on dividing power between the king and an elite group of men who would make sure the system worked for all. In *The Spirit of the Laws*, Montesquieu outlines what he believes are the proper roles for the monarch, the aristocracy, and the people.

The people, in whom the supreme power resides, ought to have the management of everything within their reach: that which exceeds their abilities must be conducted by their ministers.

But they cannot properly be said to have their ministers, without the power of nominating them: it is, therefore, a fundamental maxim in this government, that the people should choose their ministers—that is, their magistrates.

They have occasion, as well as monarchs, and even more so, to be directed by a council or senate. But to have a proper confidence in these, they should have the choosing of the members; whether the election be made by themselves, as at Athens, or by some deputed for that purpose, as on certain occasions was customary at Rome.

To Montesquieu, this separation of powers ensured a flexible political system that was stable yet capable of changing to prevent abuses of power. He also stressed that law is based on a tension between two pairs of opposite principles: liberty versus constraint and necessity versus freedom.

THE FATHER OF SOCIOLOGY

In *The Spirit of the Laws*, Montesquieu puts forth his rather strange climate theory. He believed that climate greatly influences each society and culture. He also argued that certain climates are superior to others, and that the moderate climate in France is the best one possible. People who lived in hot weather countries were "too hot-tempered" and people living in cold northern countries were "icy" or "stiff," he explained. The most desirable type of person was to be found in the moderate climate of central Europe.

However strange this theory is, it served Montesquieu well. With it, he showed the relationship between the character of a people and their form of government. He believed that each culture demanded a form of government and system of laws best suited to its character. The emphasis that Montesquieu placed on the role that social aspects and environmental factors, such as climate and geography, play in shaping a nation has led some scholars to call him the father of sociology.

THE ROLE OF SCIENCE

During his professional years with the Bordeaux parliament, Montesquieu had been a very active member of the Bordeaux Academy of Sciences. He was interested in biology, and he was especially drawn to vitalism, a theory that supported the existence of vital forces in living organisms. Organisms, vitalists argued, did not work like machines, but instead were constantly

Montesquieu wears a judge's robe in this portrait, probably during his time as president of the Bordeaux parliament. As a member of the parliament, Montesquieu learned a great deal about law and government. He would put this knowledge to good use in his most famous book, *The Spirit of the Laws*.

changing in order to maintain their best form possible—that of a well-regulated, balanced entity.

Montesquieu translated this scientific concept as the idea of checks and balances in his political theory. According to this idea, the separate branches within a government should constantly exert a force on each other, producing a dynamic but balanced system. Montesquieu's ideal government was one that was vital, alive, and responsive to needs and pressures. Such a system, he believed, would remain strong and stable, and produce a government that is much better suited to human needs than the rigid forms of absolutism.

THE FINAL TOUCHES

Treating his masterpiece very much like a changing, adapting organism, striving for improvement and balance, Montesquieu continued to make additions and edits to *The Spirit of the Laws* during his last days in his library at La Brède. His dedication to the project clearly proves how important the book was to Montesquieu. As the years passed, it would become an equally important book to many other people.

ENLIGHTENMENT AND THE REVOLUTIONS

CHAPTER 5

1
2
3
4
5
6

Montesquieu, like the other leaders of the Enlightenment, was interested in human relationships with the natural world. John Locke (1632–1704), a political theorist whose ideas greatly influenced the American concept of government, saw nature as a creative and positive influence. He believed that a government's role was to model society after the state of nature. This shows a shift from the Renaissance view of nature as a chaotic force to the early Enlightenment concept of nature as an orderly system. Ironically, however, the attempt to reorder the world according to this new rational and gentler order led to revolution.

At the end of the eighteenth century, major social and economic changes were taking place across

Europe. Many people were critical of government, feeling it was unable or unwilling to adapt to these changes. Montesquieu's writings contributed to the call for revolution that was spreading across the world. The French Revolution and the American Revolution are the two most important events that were fueled by Enlightenment principles.

ENGLAND'S EXAMPLE

When Montesquieu visited England from 1729 to 1731, he came face to face with a political system that was to greatly influence his search for improved forms of government. During his two years in England, he lived in the capital city of London and led a remarkably active life. He joined the Freemasons, attended parliament debates, and was elected to the Royal Society of London. His

This portrait of John Locke was created in the late seventeenth century. Locke was an English philosopher who had beliefs similar to Montesquieu's. He is especially well known for his theory about how people can learn from experience and their senses. This theory is known as empiricism. Like Montesquieu, Locke also had a tremendous influence on political philosophy. The Founding Fathers of the United States borrowed many of Locke's ideas to draft the Constitution and Declaration of Independence.

observations and participation convinced him that the rule of law and the preservation of freedom—the two principles he saw as indispensable parts of human existence—could coexist. To Montesquieu, the English constitutional monarchy was the practical application of the Enlightenment's ideals of freedom, tolerance, moderation, and reason.

UNREST IN THE FRENCH PARLIAMENT

For much of the eighteenth century, French political conflicts involved attempts of French parliament to gain constitutional powers equal to those granted to the British parliament. But the French parliament was radically different than that of England. There were no elected officials in the French parliament. Instead, a French parliament seat was considered private property. Much like a family home, these seats were passed on through inheritance or sold for cash if the need arose. Operating on such a model, the French political system found itself unable to respond to demands for reform. It soon became obvious that Montesquieu's grand ideal of a French version of British government would not become reality without radical changes within the French political structure. At the end of the century the whole system exploded in the great French Revolution of 1789.

This painting depicts a gathering of the French parliament during the eighteenth century. Wealthy and influential members of French society dominated Parliament. One of the causes of the French Revolution was the tension between the members of Parliament and the middle-class citizens of France who wished for more influence in government.

THE FRENCH REVOLUTION

The French Revolution of 1789 began, true to Montesquieu's legacy, in a spirit of reform, but it was soon taken over by extremism and violence. For some intellectuals, a government by enlightened despotism was a desirable form of rule, especially when compared to weaker political systems. By the end of the eighteenth century, however, the flaws in any type of absolutist government, even an enlightened one, were becoming apparent, and reformers began to call for new political systems. More and more people began calling for the separation of powers as a protection against the abuse of kings and queens. In this way, the theory that Montesquieu offered in *The Spirit of the Laws* significantly influenced European history.

THE FRENCH REVOLUTION'S DEBT TO THE ENLIGHTENMENT

Many factors led to the French Revolution. Financial crises, social stresses, and economic problems all contributed. Along with these conditions, Enlightenment ideals and values provided the inspiration and directions for various revolutionary groups.

On August 4, 1789, a group of noblemen and bourgeois delegates declared a reduction in the power of wealthy landowners, thereby beginning the French Revolution. Using Montesquieu's writings as inspiration, the group of reformers intended their movement to be a moderate one. The August 4 declaration was meant to ensure that all French men (women were not included in the declaration), regardless of their social status or wealth, would be treated equally by law.

The conflict grew worse not only among the opposition, those who were losing their feudal privileges, but also among other groups who began to demand

Première SCENE de la RÉVOLUTION Française A PARIS.

Le 12 Juillet 1789, on apprit à Paris que le Roi renvoyoit M.ʳ Necker; Les Factieux qui n'attendoient qu'une occasion pour éclater saisir celle-là, et firent agir leurs agents, les quels Suivis d'une foule de peuple qu'ils avoient amassé, parcoururent les divers quartiers de la Ville, excitant les citoyens à la révolte; L'un d'eux montant sur une borne haranguait le peuple, tenant les discours les plus Séditieux.; On portoit les Bustes du Duc d'Orléans, et de M.ʳ Necker; l'après midi ils furent à tous les théatres faire cesser les Spectacles.

This illustration depicts a demonstration against the government in Paris on July 12, 1789. Two days later, a Parisian mob stormed the Bastille, killing a government official and releasing a number of prisoners. Some historians believe that these events marked the beginning of the French Revolution, while others believe the Revolution officially began with the declaration of August 4.

more radical and immediate changes in government. As a result, the declaration of August 4, 1789, made the political crisis in France extremely unstable and set the stage for rebellion.

The revolutionaries who demanded a change of government struggled to reach an agreement on what the new form of government would be. Moderate thinkers, following Montesquieu's lead, wanted to retain the monarchy but transform it into a limited and constitutional monarchy modeled after England. Other groups called for a republic in

THE QUESTION OF EQUALITY

Leaders of the French Revolution used Enlightenment political theory for both general ideals and vocabulary. The famous slogan of the French Revolution—*liberté, egalité, et fraternité* (liberty, equality, and brotherhood)—was taken directly from Enlightenment belief in the universal qualities of human nature.

Many Enlightenment philosophers believed that equality was the natural condition of humankind. Political institutions, then, should work to preserve this natural condition. Unfortunately, although the philosophers at the time wished to apply their ideas to society, problems arose

This calendar from 1794 includes a variation on the slogan of the French Revolution, Liberté, Egalité, Fraternité, ou La Mort *(Liberty, Equality, Brotherhood, or Death.)*

when people began trying to give the French Revolution's values concrete forms of existence. They could not agree on specific reforms and political structures. What, exactly, did equality mean? Did it have a different meaning in politics than it did in economics? Were men and women truly equal? The search for answers to these questions led to some of the most radical changes in human history.

which elected officials would rule the nation. A small group of radical reformers insisted that direct democracy was the only way to govern France.

As often happens after a revolution, none of the new political groups in France were able to establish authority in any lasting way. Social discontent, war, political opposition, and economic hardship led to chaos in France. As each group attempted to take hold of the leadership of France, it began resorting to terror and intimidation in order to establish itself and to protect itself from enemies, both real and imagined.

NAPOLÉON BONAPARTE

The turmoil caused by the revolution in France was finally brought under control by Napoléon Bonaparte

(1769–1821), a brilliant military strategist and officer in the French army. In addition to being a great leader, Napoléon was also an extremely well-read man. Among his favorite works was Montesquieu's *The Spirit of the Laws*, which he studied during his early years as a military officer and read often as he grew older.

Napoléon was a fitting example of a man of the Enlightenment. His devotion to Enlightenment ideals was such that when he led the French army into war against Egypt, he brought scholars along with him. This led to the unearthing of the Rosetta Stone, among many other discoveries. Under his leadership, France went to war with many other European nations and soon took control of much of Europe. As a result, Enlightenment thought and writing spread throughout Europe.

Napoléon assumed control of France in 1799 as first consul, then declared himself emperor of

Napoléon Bonaparte poses in his military uniform in this portrait from 1803. The year after this portrait was done, Napoléon would crown himself emperor of France. Napoléon is one of the most famous figures in the history of France. During his lifetime, France conquered large parts of Europe while making sweeping changes to French government and society. Napoléon's rise to power, however, came crashing down when his army was defeated by the British at Waterloo in 1815.

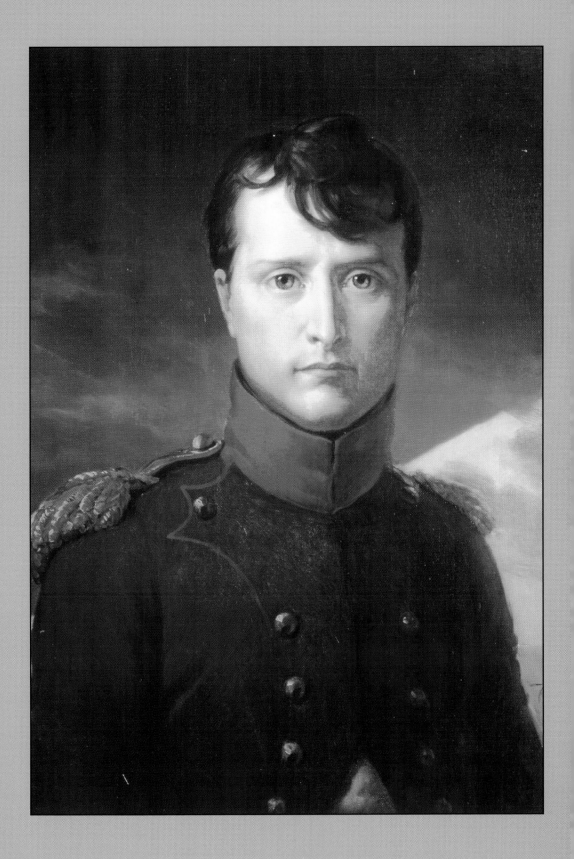

WATER AND THE METRIC SYSTEM

The metric system was invented by French scientists in the mid-seventeenth century. It spread throughout Europe during the 1789 French Revolution. In accordance with the Enlightenment's celebration of human reason, the metric system provided a better way for

people to communicate with each other by establishing common units of length, volume, mass, and temperature.

The metric unit of length is one meter and was originally defined as equal to 1/40,000,000 of Earth's circumference. Today, however, one meter is defined as the distance traveled by light in a

This illustration from 1795 demonstrates various ways in which the metric system could be used. The illustration is entitled Use of the New Measurements *(Usage des Nouvelle Mesures).*

vacuum in a time interval of 1/299,792,458 of a second. The unit of mass (kilogram) is based on the amount of water contained in a cube with sides one decimeter (one-tenth of a meter) long, under specific conditions. The metric unit of volume (liter) is based on the volume of water contained in such a cube. Celsius, the metric measurement of temperature, is based on a reading of water freezing at 0 degrees and boiling at 100 degrees. Freezing and boiling temperatures for all other materials are measured in relation to the freezing and boiling temperatures of water.

Based on multiples of ten, the metric system provides a quick and easy way to do calculations of length, volume, mass, and temperature. Most countries today use the metric system. The United States and Britain, however, have chosen to remain with the British, or imperial, system of measurements.

France in 1804, when he also became known as Napoléon I or Napoléon le Grand (the Great). He instituted many laws based on Montesquieu's ideas of legal and political equality. Under his rule, public office was no longer considered private property. Instead, public officials were hired by the state and paid on the basis of their talents. The Napoleonic Code was instituted to provide every French citizen with access to the same laws. Free enterprise and private property also became legally protected for the first time. Napoléon is the classic example of an enlightened despot. Although there were no impediments to his quests for personal gain, he worked for the good of his people and his country.

REVOLUTION FROM FRANCE TO AMERICA

The issues that define the Enlightenment, such as the relationship between ideas and actions, between economic and political systems, as well as the conditions that led to radical revolution in nations, are all indebted to Montesquieu's *The Spirit of the Laws*. This book was a driving force for both Enlightenment ideals and the resulting demands for revolutions.

James Madison (1751–1836) was not yet born when *The Spirit of the Laws* was first translated into English in 1750. At that time, Great Britain's colonies in North America were part of the British Empire and proud of it. However, within twenty years, the colonies would begin to disagree with many of the policies of the British government.

When Americans began to grow restless under the distant rule of England, Montesquieu's writings provided them with a framework of ideas that they could use to give direction to their grievances and their goals. At the time, there had not yet been a nation anywhere in the world with a written constitution. Montesquieu's *The Spirit of the Laws* was the closest anyone had come to creating a written version of the rules for a republic. This would serve as the basis of a first draft for future constitution makers in America.

MADISON AND MONTESQUIEU

James Madison studied Montesquieu's work at Princeton University in New Jersey. Twenty years after leaving college, he could still quote whole paragraphs from memory. Madison expanded on Montesquieu's idea of a republic by insisting that the very nature of a group of states united in a republic was cause enough for stability. Madison stated his thoughts on this topic in the Federalist Papers, a series of newspaper articles published in New York City, from 1787 to 1788, to explain the new constitution to readers. In the Federalist Papers, Madison stated that the diversity of the states would give "a republican remedy for the diseases most incident to republican government." What Madison was saying is that since the territories of the states were so large and their populations so diverse, abuses of power would be unlikely to occur. As one group of people increased in power, a different group would rise up to counter and keep them from becoming too powerful.

SEPARATION OF POWERS

Montesquieu favored compromise in his politics. Like the American leaders who had won the revolution and whom he had greatly influenced, he hated extremes. When those leaders met to draft the U.S. Constitution, their first concern was to set up a system that would work to ensure peace and freedom. Everyone involved did not want to see a repeat of the revolution's bloody struggle for freedom.

Because Montesquieu was suspicious of human nature, he believed that anyone who held power would most likely want more power. The only way to work against this basic human failure was to set up a system of government based on competing powers. Madison and the rest of the Founding Fathers, wishing above all to avoid tyranny of any kind, thoroughly subscribed to Montesquieu's theory on the separation of powers into legislative, executive, and judicial branches.

Montesquieu always had his eye on the matter of fact. His ideas may have been revolutionary, but he was never a revolutionary himself. He believed freedom was something that grew gradually out of the history of a country, not something that could be imposed by one group of people on another. "Political liberty," he wrote in *The Spirit of the Laws*, "consists in security; or, at least, in the opinion that we enjoy security."

Montesquieu did not believe that people left to themselves would naturally strive to improve the human race. His historical studies had taught him how efficient and long-lasting despotism based on pure terror and violence could be. His view of political systems relied on human reason and freedom, though not human goodness, as its ideals. Ideas of universal liberty and absolute power for the people meant mob rule to Montesquieu. In *The Spirit of the Laws*, he states that direct rule by the people will lead to a tyranny far worse than any king's. To Montesquieu, small groups of elite and wise men acting as intermediaries between the people and the head of state and the resulting competition between those groups was the only way to prevent a tyrannical government. The U.S. political system of representative democracy would be built directly upon the recommendations in Montesquieu's *The Spirit of the Laws*.

REVOLUTION IN AMERICA

In the eighteenth century, Britain, which claimed sovereignty over the American colonies, made harsh attempts to control colonial behavior. Legislation such as the Stamp Act (1765) and the Declaratory Act (1766), in which England claimed far-reaching powers, were widely condemned throughout the colonies. When British legislation restricted the powers of the colonial representatives and strengthened those of the governor appointed by the British king, the conflict between the colonies and Britain became even more extreme. Tensions over British policies caused colonial demands for independence to grow stronger every day. In April 1775, the first skirmishes of the American Revolution broke out at Lexington and Concord in Massachusetts.

In the years leading to this event, American colonial leaders drew on the European Enlightenment for political theories and principles. In addition to supplying its Enlightenment ideals to the American effort, France lent its military might to the struggle against English rule. The French fleet arrived in North American waters in 1778 and contributed to the English defeat in 1781. With the 1783 Treaty of Paris, Britain formally recognized the independence of the United States of America.

On December 16, 1773, British colonists in America staged the Boston Tea Party. Disguised as Native Americans, a group of about sixty men boarded three ships loaded with tea and tossed the cargo overboard. The demonstration was a protest against the Tea Act of 1773, a law passed by the British government that the colonists felt was unfair.

Once free from English rule, American leaders set about incorporating the principles of the Enlightenment into the constitution of their new nation. The United States Constitution based the new government on Enlightenment principles: the separation of powers, and religious tolerance. In accordance with the writings in *The Spirit of the Laws*, it formally established a separation of church and state, and granted basic rights such as life, liberty, and the pursuit of happiness, which were hallmarks of

"WHAT IS ENLIGHTENMENT?"

In 1784, Immanuel Kant (1724–1804), a German philosopher and a major contributor to Enlightenment thought, wrote a short essay entitled "What Is Enlightenment?" In it, he praised human reason as the way to freedom and knowledge:

> Enlightenment is man's release from his self-incurred tutelage. Tutelage is man's ability to make use of his understanding without direction from another. Self-incurred is this tutelage when its cause lies not in lack of reason but in lack of resolution and courage to use it without direction from another. *Sapere aude!* "have courage to use your own reason"—that is the motto of Enlightenment.

Enlightenment thought. Montesquieu was widely quoted in the flurry of newspaper articles that were published to explain the new constitution to the people and to persuade the states to ratify it. He remains the most widely cited source in those articles, quoted three times more than the philosopher John Locke, the second most-cited source.

The success of the American Revolution created great excitement in Europe, where the American experiment was discussed and analyzed. The American Revolution was seen as the first direct and successful application of the Enlightenment ideals of freedom, brotherhood, and equality. It seemed to these observers that the American Revolution was validating their Enlightenment ideals and dreams about human potential. The American Revolution, then, not only gave birth to the United States, but also served as a symbol of the Enlightenment.

MONTESQUIEU TODAY

Democratic government is the favored type of government in modern times. Other forms of rule, such as monarchy, or aristocracy, are considered naturally illegitimate or unjust, regardless of how the rulers actually govern. Like most Western thinkers before him, Montesquieu did not think much of a democratic form of government. While believing that every man was entitled to freedom and equal protection under the law, he did not believe that every man was capable of ruling, and women had even less status in his writings. Proper government needed qualified citizens, and in Montesquieu's eyes most people were not intelligent, wealthy, or experienced enough to rule wisely.

Instead, Montesquieu preferred to place the responsibility of ruling in the hands of a small, elite group. This group was adult, male, wealthy, and educated. In his opinion, the elite best understood the way to govern. He believed that people are basically and universally self-serving and power-hungry, and recommended that only limited political power be given to any one ruler or group. This is the basis for his idea of the separation of powers, in which the government is broken into separate legislative, executive, and judicial

James Madison (1751–1836) incorporated Montesquieu's ideas into the Constitution. Later, he would become the fourth president of the United States (1809–1817).

branches. A fair government, he argued, ensured the protection of all and rule for the common good, but he believed neither despotism nor democracy were the forms suited to such a goal.

Montesquieu's pessimistic view of human nature was very much in keeping with eighteenth-century political thinkers. James Madison, the leading drafter of the U.S. Constitution, agreed that a democracy that protected the rights of everyone, not just the majority, was necessary to prevent an individual or a

BY ALL THE PEOPLE, FOR ALL THE PEOPLE

The United States government is a representative democracy, a modern form of Montesquieu's ideal republican form of rule. From the time it became a nation, the United States has been grappling with questions about who should be granted the full rights of citizenship. Since two main goals of governing by democracy are to prevent dictatorship or tyranny and to promote social and moral well-being, the United States has, over time, extended

full rights to all its adult citizens. This is one of the points at which the United States departs from Montesquieu, who referred primarily to a small group of wealthy and educated men in his political writing.

Montesquieu had very little to say about women. He

Pictured above is Marie de Vichy-Chamrond, marquise du Deffand (1697–1780), a writer and salon hostess in Paris.

described women as weak, calm, and gentle. He wrote that such traits made it impossible for women to control a household. This might give the indication that women did not contribute very much to the Enlightenment movement. Everyday reality, however, painted a very different picture. Women regularly took part in Enlightenment discussions. Eighteenth-century intellectual activity in France often took place in salons, where a society hostess would invite a group of people to share gossip and discuss new ideas in philosophy and politics. A handful of these hostesses became famous for their ability to lead discussions, pull delicate political strings, and sidestep political obstacles, such as censorship of written Enlightenment theories. The salon hostesses also worked to get several philosophers appointed to important positions within the government.

group from becoming too powerful. Madison and Montesquieu both thought that the unavoidable human problems of personal greed and ambition could even serve as the basis of good government. They believed that if government were divided into separate groups with each one's interests at odds with the others, a system of checks and balances would be set up that would prevent any one group from becoming too powerful. The U.S. government's three branches—executive, judicial, and legislative—were created so that each would check the other's natural greed for more power, and, therefore, prevent tyranny.

ENLIGHTENMENT IN THE UNITED STATES

The new nation of the United States of America came into being with the colonies' 1776 Declaration of Independence, in which they claimed their right to self-government. Some of the major cities in the eighteenth-century United States, especially Philadelphia, had cultural and intellectual lives that closely reflected the European cities of the Enlightenment. When the Founding Fathers of the United States came together to draft a constitution for their new nation, they came well versed in Enlightenment writings, including those of Montesquieu.

During the European Enlightenment, Montesquieu and others relied on the written word to make ideas legitimate. This was true in the United States, also. Inspired by Montesquieu, James Madison, along with other Founding Fathers, wrote a series of eighty-five essays in defense of the proposed constitution. These essays were published as *The Federalist Papers* (1788), and they heavily cited Montes-quieu's *The Spirit of the Laws* throughout their pages. *The Federalist Papers* are considered classic Enlightenment political theory.

In the process of creating the new nation, American leaders of the Enlightenment had the chance to put their ideas into action. They constructed their new government on a foun-dation provided by such concepts as natural

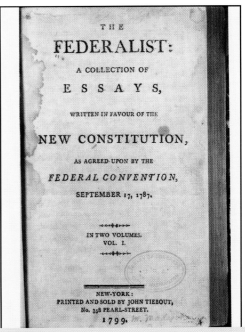

Above is the title page from the first volume of *The Federalist: A Collection of Essays, Written in Favor of the New Constitution*, also known as *The Federalist Papers*.

rights, equality, happiness, toleration, separation of powers, freedom, and separation of church and state. All of these concepts were taken directly from Montesquieu's work and reflected the goals of the Enlightenment movement.

IN EUROPE

For Europeans of the Enlightenment, the events that unfolded in North America raised hopes that

The Declaration of the Rights of Man and of the Citizen was a document created in 1789 by the people behind the French Revolution. The declaration consists of a list of seventeen rights that a just government should protect among its citizens. Many of the principles are similar to ones found in the United States' Bill of Rights and Declaration of Independence. Seen above is a symbolic painting, also created in 1789, in which the declaration is engraved on a stone monument. In the background is an eye within a triangle of light. The light symbolizes wisdom, or knowledge, which illuminates the rights of man.

fundamental changes could occur in their societies. Most important, America provided a model of a constitution with which to test conflicting ideas about how best to realize Enlightenment principles. As such, the Constitution was both praised and criticized in Europe.

The Constitution established a federal republic in the United States, which was structured according to Montesquieu's principle of the separation of powers. This republic was to be run as a representative democracy: the people would elect government officials to represent them at both federal and local levels.

Each branch of the new American government was provided with specific duties and with powers that would balance the powers of the other branches. In addition, a conflict was set up between the interests of the federal government and that of the individual states, for which certain specific powers were preserved. Montesquieu's recommendation of a flexible, self-adjusting system was realized in the United States government's system of checks and balances. The new American nation was the concrete application of the first modern era—the European eighteenth-century movement called the Enlightenment.

MONTESQUIEU'S LEGACY

Montesquieu remains one of the most widely read and significant leaders of the Enlightenment. His books offered criticism of contemporary French society and helped to popularize the ideals of the English constitutional monarchy throughout Europe. Furthermore, his legacy in political theory, history, and sociology was one of the most important contributions of the Enlightenment to modern Western civilization.

REFORMS OF THE ENLIGHTENMENT

The Enlightenment is generally thought of as an era ruled by faith in reason, progress, individuality, universal brotherhood, and humanitarian values. But there were other aspects to the Enlightenment as well. Above all, the intellectuals of the Enlightenment believed in and tried to act on the idea that knowledge should benefit humankind. Knowledge was expected to yield results—new institutions, new practices, new technologies—all of which would contribute to society in a positive way.

The drive for practical results called for reform in all aspects of life. New political systems, such as republics and democracies; new literary forms, such

Even today, the French are immensely proud of the accomplishments of Montesquieu. In fact, their 200 franc note features a portrait of Montesquieu, as seen above. Unfortunately, France has adopted to a different type of currency (the Euro) and the Montesquieu bill will be valid only until 2008.

as the novel and literary journals; and new ideas about commerce and business, such as laissez-faire economics, are all results of Enlightenment's search for the best possible society.

ABUSE OF ENLIGHTENMENT IDEAS

A primary Enlightenment idea was that human reason was the source of morality as well as what made humans distinct from other creatures. This idea spread throughout Europe over many years and became a central belief of Western civilization. In some places, however, such as Nazi-led Germany, it was distorted. Nazi leaders proposed that the more rational (able to use reason) a person was thought to be, the more human that person was. This led to ideas that some people were less rational, and therefore less human, than others. From there, it was a short jump to justify any behavior on the part of the people considered superior.

Once the leaders of Nazi Germany defined themselves as superior to all other people, they set upon a course to dominate and eradicate all those they considered inferior. In their hands, rationality became equated with military might and allowed them to justify the slaughter of innocent people. Nazi leaders completely disregarded the Enlightenment view that respect for human beings is something confirmed by human reason.

TOMORROW

As the Enlightenment pressed on, the old institutions of European society disappeared or were transformed into the modern world we know now. The Enlightenment brought the modern world into being and gave it a political, social, economic, and intellectual legacy that continues to guide and shape our thinking. Today, Montesquieu's ideals provide the framework for contemporary discussions of the role and form of government. He remains one of the most influential figures of the Enlightenment and his influence shows no sign of fading.

TIMELINE

1643	Louis XIV is crowned king of France.
1689	Montesquieu is born at La Brède in Gascony, France.
1708	Montesquieu is admitted to the Bordeaux parliament.
1715	King Louis XIV dies. Montesquieu marries Jeanne de Lartigue.
1721	*Persian Letters* is published.
1728	Montesquieu becomes a member of the French Academy.
1734	*Considerations on the Causes of the Greatness of the Romans and Their Decline* is published.
1743	*The Spirit of the Laws* is completed.
1748	*The Spirit of the Laws* is published.
1751	Denis Diderot publishes the first volume of the *Encyclopedia*.
1755	Montesquieu dies in Paris.
1775–1783	The American Revolution takes place.
1784	Immanuel Kant publishes "What is Enlightenment?"
1788	The U.S. Constitution is ratified by the states.
1789	George Washington is elected the first president of the United States of America. The French Revolution begins.
1804–1814	Napoléon rules as France's first emperor.

GLOSSARY

abolition The act of doing away with.

absolutism A form of government in which all power is held by a single ruler.

aesthetics A branch of philosophy that deals with the nature of beauty.

anonymously With no name given.

aristocracy A hereditary ruling class also known as the nobility.

bourgeois Relating to the social middle class.

doctrine The fundamental belief of an organization.

dowry The money or property that a woman brings to her husband in marriage.

enlightened despotism A system of government in which the ruler has unlimited power but uses it for the good of his or her subjects.

eunuch A castrated man placed in charge of a harem.

exchequer An office responsible for the collection and management of a kingdom's money.

Founding Fathers The men who signed the Declaration of Independence, U.S. Constitution, or who played leading roles in the American Revolution.

Freemasons Members of a secret society of men named the Ancient Free and Accepted Masons.

French Academy The organization that is the authority on all issues pertaining to the French language.

genre A category of literature, music, or art defined by a particular style.

Jesuits Members of the Roman Catholic Society of Jesus, which was founded in the sixteenth century and devoted to educating people about Catholicism.

laissez-faire Belief that the government should limit its influence in certain areas, especially concerning trade and commerce.

monarchy A type of government led by a king or queen.

parliament A group of people responsible for making laws for a country, state, or city.

persecution The act of making someone suffer because of his or her beliefs.

potentate One who has great power.

ratification The official approval of a document or an idea.

Reformation A sixteenth-century movement in Europe that aimed at reforming practices of the Roman Catholic Church and resulted in the establishment of the Protestant faith.

...h citizens elect
vernment.

istian church
e pope.

799 that was used
Egyptian writing.

behavior in a

edom from control-

ent that is unfair

FOR MORE INFORMATION

American Society for Eighteenth-
  Century Studies
PO Box 7867
Wake Forest University
Winston-Salem, NC 27109
(336) 727-4694
Web site: http://asecs.press.jhu.edu

Center for Seventeenth- and Eighteenth-
  Century Studies
310 Royce Hall
UCLA
Los Angeles, California 90095-1404
(310) 206-8552
Web site: http://www.humnet.ucla.edu/
  humnet/c1718cs

The Constitution Society
7793 Burnet Road #37
Austin, TX 78757
Web site: http://www.constitution.org/
  cm/sol-02.htm

The Supreme Court of the United States
1 First Street NE
Washington, DC 20543
(202) 479-3211
Web site: http://
  www.supremecourtus.gov

TeachingAmericanHistory.Org
401 College Avenue
Ashland, OH 44805
(877) 289-5411
Web site: http://teachingamericanhistory.org

WEB SITES

Due to the changing nature of Internet links, the
Rosen Publishing Group, Inc., has developed an online
list of Web sites related to the subject of this book.
This site is updated regularly. Please use this link to
access the list:

http://www.rosenlinks.com/phen/mont

FOR FURTHER READING

Barber, Nicola. *The French Revolution.* North Mankato, MN: Smart Apple Media, 2004.

Dunn, John. *The Enlightenment.* San Diego, CA: Lucent Books, 1999.

Egendorf, Laura K., ed. *The French Revolution.* San Diego, CA: Greenhaven, 2004.

Goubert, Pierre. *The Course of French History.* New York, NY: Franklin Watts, 1998.

Huff, Toby. *An Age of Science and Revolutions, 1600–1800.* New York, NY: Oxford University Press, 2005.

Kallen, Stuart, A. *The 1700s.* Farmington Hills, MI: Greenhaven Press, 2001.

Kors, Alan Charles, ed. *Encyclopedia of the Enlightenment.* New York, NY: Oxford University Press, 2002.

Law, Stephen. *Philosophy Rocks!* New York, NY: Volo, 2002.

May, Henry F. *The Enlightenment in America.* New York, NY: Oxford University Press, 1976.

Meltzer, Milton, ed. *The American Revolutionaries: A History in Their Own Words 1750–1800.* Minneapolis, MN: Sagebrush Bound, 2000.

Montesquieu, Charles-Louis de Secondat, Baron de. *Persian Letters.* New York, NY: Penguin Books, 1972.

Montesquieu, Charles-Louis de Secondat, Baron de. *The Spirit of the Laws.* New York, NY: Cambridge University Press, 1989.

Sanford, William R. *Basic Principles of American Government.* New York, NY: Amsco, 1986.

Stimpson, Bea. *The World of Enlightenment.* Cheltenham, UK: Nelson Thornes, 1999.

BIBLIOGRAPHY

Aron, Raymond. *Main Currents in Sociological Thought.* Somerset, NJ: Transaction Publishers, 1998.

Horkheimer, Max, and Theodore Adorno. *Dialectic of Enlightenment.* Translated by John Cumming. New York, NY: Continuum International Publishing Group, 1976.

Hulliung, Mark. *Montesquieu and the Old Regime.* Berkeley, CA: University of California Press, 1976.

Iain, Stewart. "Montesquieu in England: His 'Notes on England,' with Commentary and Translation." Oxford University Comparative Law. Retrieved August 2004 (http://ouclf.iuscomp. org/articles/montesquieu.shtml).

Montesquieu, Charles-Louis de Secondat, Baron de. *Persian Letters.* New York, NY: Penguin Books, 1972.

Montesquieu, Charles-Louis de Secondat, Baron de. *The Spirit of the Laws.* New York, NY: Cambridge University Press, 1989.

Shackleton, Robert. *Montesquieu: A Critical Biography.* London, UK: Oxford University Press, 1961.

Sparks, Christopher. *Montesquieu's Vision of Uncertainty and Modernity in Political Philosophy.* Lampeter, UK: The Edwin Mellen Press, 1999.

Wernick, Robert. "The Godfather of the American Constitution." *Smithsonian*, Vol. 20, No. 6, September 1989, p. 183.

Wikipedia. "Encyclopédie."Retrieved January 2005 (http://en.wikipedia.org/wiki/Encyclopedie).

Wikipedia. "The Age of Enlightenment." Retrieved January 2005 (http://en.wikipedia.org/wiki/The_Age_of_Enlightenment).

INDEX

ABOUT THE AUTHOR

Susan Gordon is an editor of social studies workbooks at a major educational publisher in New York City. She earned her MFA in creative writing at New School University, and her BA at Temple University, where she studied English, Italian, and French literature and criticism.

CREDITS